THE FOUR
AGREEMENTS

Also by don Miguel Ruiz

THE MASTERY OF LOVE
A Practical Guide to the Art of Relationship

THE FOUR AGREEMENTS COMPANION BOOK
Using the Four Agreements to Master the Dream of Your Life

THE FOUR AGREEMENTS AUDIO
Read by actor Peter Coyote

PRAYERS
A Communion with our Creator

THE VOICE OF KNOWLEDGE
A Practical Guide to Inner Peace

LOS CUATRO ACUERDOS
Una guía práctica para la libertad personal

CUADERNO DE TRABAJO DE LOS CUATRO ACUERDOS
Utiliza los Cuatro Acuerdos para gobernar el sueño de tu vida

LA MAESTRÍA DEL AMOR
Una guía práctica para el arte de las relaciones

ORACIONES
Una comunión con nuestro Creador

LA VOZ DEL CONOCIMIENTO
Una guía práctica para la paz interior

To the *Circle of Fire*;
those who have gone before,
those who are present,
and those who have yet to come.

Contents

A Practical Guide to Personal Freedom

A

Toltec

THE FOUR
AGREEMENTS

Wisdom
Book

DON MIGUEL RUIZ

AMBER-ALLEN PUBLISHING
SAN RAFAEL, CALIFORNIA

Copyright © 1997 by Miguel Angel Ruiz, M.D.

Published by Amber-Allen Publishing, Inc.
Post Office Box 6657
San Rafael, California 94903

Editorial: Janet Mills
Cover Illustration: Nicholas Wilton
Cover Design: Michele Wetherbee
Author Photo: Ellen Denuto

Note: The term "black magic" is not meant to convey racial connotation; it
is merely used to describe the use of magic for adverse or harmful purposes.

Library of Congress Cataloging-in-Publication Data
Ruiz, Miguel, 1952– The four agreements : a practical guide to personal
freedom/Miguel Ruiz. p. cm. — (A Toltec wisdom book) (alk. paper)
I. Conduct of life.   2. Toltec philosophy — Miscellanea.
I. Title.   II. Series: Ruiz, Miguel, 1952– Toltec wisdom book.
BJ1581. 2. R85 1997   299'.792 — dc21   97-18256 CIP

ISBN I-878424-31-9
Printed in Canada on acid-free paper
Distributed by Publishers Group West

46   45   44   43   42   41   40   39

Acknowledgments

I WOULD LIKE TO HUMBLY ACKNOWLEDGE MY mother Sarita, who taught me unconditional love; my father Jose Luis, who taught me discipline; my grandfather Leonardo Macias, who gave me the key to unlock the Toltec mysteries; and my sons Miguel, Jose Luis, and Leonardo.

I wish to express my deep affection and appreciation to the dedication of Gaya Jenkins and Trey Jenkins.

I would like to extend my profound gratitude to Janet Mills — publisher, editor, believer. I am also abidingly grateful to Ray Chambers for lighting the way.

Acknowledgments

I would like to honor my dear friend Gini Gentry, an amazing "brain" whose faith touched my heart.

I would like to pay tribute to the many people who have given freely of their time, hearts, and resources to support the teachings. A partial list includes: Gae Buckley, Ted and Peggy Raess, Christinea Johnson, Judy "Red" Fruhbauer, Vicki Molinar, David and Linda Dibble, Bernadette Vigil, Cynthia Wootton, Alan Clark, Rita Rivera, Catherine Chase, Stephanie Bureau, Todd Kaprielian, Glenna Quigley, Allan and Randi Hardman, Cindee Pascoe, Tink and Chuck Cowgill, Roberto and Diane Paez, Siri Gian Singh Khalsa, Heather Ash, Larry Andrews, Judy Silver, Carolyn Hipp, Kim Hofer, Mersedeh Kheradmand, Diana and Sky Ferguson, Keri Kropidlowski, Steve Hasenburg, Dara Salour, Joaquin Galvan, Woodie Bobb, Rachel Guerrero, Mark Gershon, Collette Michaan, Brandt Morgan, Katherine Kilgore (Kitty Kaur), Michael Gilardy, Laura Haney, Marc Cloptin, Wendy Bobb, Ed Fox,

Acknowledgments

Yari Jaeda, Mary Carroll Nelson, Amari Magdelana, JaneAnn Dow, Russ Venable, Gu and Maya Khalsa, Mataji Rosita, Fred and Marion Vatinelli, Diane Laurent, V.J. Polich, Gail Dawn Price, Barbara Simon, Patti Torres, Kaye Thompson, Ramin Yazdani, Linda Lightfoot, Terry Gorton, Dorothy Lee, J.J. Frank, Jennifer and Jeanne Jenkins, George Gorton, Tita Weems, Shelley Wolf, Gigi Boyce, Morgan Drasmin, Eddie Von Sonn, Sydney de Jong, Peg Hackett Cancienne, Germaine Bautista, Pilar Mendoza, Debbie Rund Caldwell, Bea La Scalla, Eduardo Rabasa, and The Cowboy.

The Toltec

THOUSANDS OF YEARS AGO, THE TOLTEC WERE known throughout southern Mexico as "women and men of knowledge." Anthropologists have spoken of the Toltec as a nation or a race, but, in fact, the Toltec were scientists and artists who formed a society to explore and conserve the spiritual knowledge and practices of the ancient ones. They came together as masters *(naguals)* and students at Teotihuacan, the ancient city of pyramids outside Mexico City known as the place where "Man Becomes God."

Over the millennia, the *naguals* were forced to conceal the ancestral wisdom and maintain its existence in obscurity. European conquest, coupled with rampant misuse of personal power by a few of the apprentices, made it necessary to shield the knowledge from those who were not prepared to use it wisely or who might intentionally misuse it for personal gain.

Fortunately, the esoteric Toltec knowledge was embodied and passed on through generations by different lineages of *naguals*. Though it remained veiled in secrecy for hundreds of years, ancient prophecies foretold the coming of an age when it would be necessary to return the wisdom to the people. Now, don Miguel Ruiz, a *nagual* from the Eagle Knight lineage, has been guided to share with us the powerful teachings of the Toltec.

Toltec knowledge arises from the same essential unity of truth as all the sacred esoteric traditions found around the world. Though it is not a religion, it honors all the spiritual masters who have taught on the earth. While it does embrace spirit, it is most accurately described as a way of life, distinguished by the ready accessibility of happiness and love.

INTRODUCTION

The Smokey Mirror

THREE THOUSAND YEARS AGO, THERE WAS A HUMAN just like you and me who lived near a city surrounded by mountains. The human was studying to become a medicine man, to learn the knowledge of his ancestors, but he didn't completely agree with everything he was learning. In his heart, he felt there must be something more.

One day, as he slept in a cave, he dreamed that he saw his own body sleeping. He came out of the cave on the night of a new moon. The sky was clear, and he could see millions of stars. Then something happened inside of him that transformed his life forever. He looked at his hands, he felt his body, and he heard his own voice say, "I am made of light; I am made of stars."

He looked at the stars again, and he realized that it's not the stars that create light, but rather light that creates the stars. "Everything is made of light," he said, "and the space in-between isn't empty." And he knew that everything that exists is one living being, and that light is the messenger of life, because it is alive and contains all information.

Then he realized that although he was made of stars, he was not those stars. "I am in-between the stars," he thought. So he called the stars the *tonal* and the light between the stars the *nagual,* and he knew that what created the harmony and space between the two is Life or Intent. Without Life, the *tonal* and the *nagual* could not exist. Life is the force of the absolute, the supreme, the Creator who creates everything.

This is what he discovered: Everything in existence is a manifestation of the one living being we call God. Everything is God. And he came to the conclusion that human perception is merely light perceiving light. He also saw that matter is a mirror — everything is a mirror that reflects light and creates images of that light — and the world of illusion, the *Dream*, is just like smoke which doesn't allow us to see what we really are. "The real us is pure love, pure light," he said.

This realization changed his life. Once he knew what he really was, he looked around at other humans and the rest of nature, and he was amazed at what he saw. He saw himself in everything — in every human, in every animal, in every tree, in the water, in the rain, in the clouds, in the earth. And he saw that Life mixed the *tonal* and the *nagual* in different ways to create billions of manifestations of Life.

In those few moments he comprehended everything. He was very excited, and his heart was filled with peace. He could hardly wait to tell his people what he had discovered. But there were no words to explain it. He tried to tell the others, but they could not understand. They could see that he had changed, that something beautiful was radiating from his eyes and his voice. They noticed that he no longer had judgment about anything or anyone. He was no longer like anyone else.

He could understand everyone very well, but no one could understand him. They believed that he was an incarnation of God, and he smiled when he heard this and he said, "It is true. I am God. But you are also God. We are the same, you and I. We are images of light. We are God." But still the people didn't understand him.

He had discovered that he was a mirror for the rest of the people, a mirror in which he could see himself. "Everyone is a mirror," he said. He saw himself in everyone, but nobody saw him as themselves.

And he realized that everyone was dreaming, but without awareness, without knowing what they really are. They couldn't see him as themselves because there was a wall of fog or smoke between the mirrors. And that wall of fog was made by the interpretation of images of light — the *Dream* of humans.

Then he knew that he would soon forget all that he had learned. He wanted to remember all the visions he had had, so he decided to call himself the Smokey Mirror so that he would always know that matter is a mirror and the smoke in-between is what keeps us from knowing what we are. He said, "I am the Smokey Mirror, because I am looking at myself in all of you, but we don't recognize each other because of the smoke in-between us. That smoke is the *Dream*, and the mirror is you, the dreamer."

Living is easy with eyes closed,
misunderstanding all you see. . . .
— John Lennon

1

Domestication and the Dream of the Planet

WHAT YOU ARE SEEING AND HEARING RIGHT NOW IS nothing but a dream. You are dreaming right now in this moment. You are dreaming with the brain awake.

Dreaming is the main function of the mind, and the mind dreams twenty-four hours a day. It dreams when the brain is awake, and it also dreams when the brain is asleep. The difference is that when the brain is awake, there is a material frame that makes us perceive things in a linear way. When we go to sleep we do not have the frame, and the dream has the tendency to change constantly.

Humans are dreaming all the time. Before we were born the humans before us created a big outside dream that we will call society's dream or *the dream of the planet.* The dream of the planet is the collective dream of billions of smaller, personal dreams, which together create a dream of a family, a dream of a community, a dream of a city, a dream of a country, and finally a dream of the whole humanity. The dream of the planet includes all of society's rules, its beliefs, its laws, its religions, its different cultures and ways to be, its governments, schools, social events, and holidays.

We are born with the capacity to learn how to dream, and the humans who live before us teach us how to dream the way society dreams. The outside dream has so many rules that when a new human is born, we hook the child's attention and introduce these rules into his or her mind. The outside dream uses Mom and Dad, the schools, and religion to teach us how to dream.

Attention is the ability we have to discriminate and to focus only on that which we want to perceive. We can perceive millions of things simultaneously, but using our attention, we can hold whatever we want to perceive in the foreground of our mind. The adults around us hooked our attention and put information into our minds through repetition. That is the way we learned everything we know.

By using our attention we learned a whole reality, a whole dream. We learned how to behave in society: what to believe and what not to believe; what is acceptable and what is not acceptable; what is good and what is bad; what is beautiful and what is ugly; what is right and what is wrong. It was all there already — all that knowledge, all those rules and concepts about how to behave in the world.

When you were in school, you sat in a little chair and put your attention on what the teacher was teaching you. When you went to church, you put your attention on what the priest or minister was telling you. It is the same dynamic with Mom and Dad, brothers and sisters: They were all trying to hook your attention. We also learn to hook the attention of other humans, and we develop a need for attention which can become very competitive. Children compete for the attention of their parents, their teachers, their friends. "Look at me! Look at what I'm doing! Hey, I'm here." The need for attention becomes very strong and continues into adulthood.

The outside dream hooks our attention and teaches us what to believe, beginning with the language that we speak. Language is the code for understanding and communication between humans. Every letter, every word in each language is an agreement. We call this a page in a book; the word *page* is an agreement that we understand. Once we understand the code, our attention is hooked and the energy is transferred from one person to another.

It was not your choice to speak English. You

didn't choose your religion or your moral values —
they were already there before you were born. We
never had the opportunity to choose what to believe
or what not to believe. We never chose even the
smallest of these agreements. We didn't even choose
our own name.

As children, we didn't have the opportunity to
choose our beliefs, but we *agreed* with the information that was passed to us from the dream of the
planet via other humans. The only way to store
information is by agreement. The outside dream
may hook our attention, but if we don't agree, we
don't store that information. As soon as we agree,
we *believe* it, and this is called faith. To have faith is
to believe unconditionally.

That's how we learn as children. Children
believe everything adults say. We agree with them,
and our faith is so strong that the belief system
controls our whole dream of life. We didn't choose
these beliefs, and we may have rebelled against them,
but we were not strong enough to win the rebellion.

The result is surrender to the beliefs with our *agreement.*

I call this process *the domestication of humans.* And through this domestication we learn how to live and how to dream. In human domestication, the information from the outside dream is conveyed to the inside dream, creating our whole belief system. First the child is taught the names of things: Mom, Dad, milk, bottle. Day by day, at home, at school, at church, and from television, we are told how to live, what kind of behavior is acceptable. The outside dream teaches us how to be a human. We have a whole concept of what a "woman" is and what a "man" is. And we also learn to judge: We judge ourselves, judge other people, judge the neighbors.

Children are domesticated the same way that we domesticate a dog, a cat, or any other animal. In order to teach a dog we punish the dog and we give it rewards. We train our children whom we love so much the same way that we train any domesticated animal: with a system of punishment and reward.

We are told, "You're a good boy," or "You're a good girl," when we do what Mom and Dad want us to do. When we don't, we are "a bad girl" or "a bad boy."

When we went against the rules we were punished; when we went along with the rules we got a reward. We were punished many times a day, and we were also rewarded many times a day. Soon we became afraid of being punished and also afraid of not receiving the reward. The reward is the attention that we got from our parents or from other people like siblings, teachers, and friends. We soon develop a need to hook other people's attention in order to get the reward.

The reward feels good, and we keep doing what others want us to do in order to get the reward. With that fear of being punished and that fear of not getting the reward, we start pretending to be what we are not, just to please others, just to be good enough for someone else. We try to please Mom and Dad, we try to please the teachers at school, we try to please the church, and so we start acting. We pretend to be what we are not because we are afraid of being rejected. The fear of being rejected becomes the fear of not being good enough. Eventually we become someone that we are not. We become a copy of Mamma's beliefs, Daddy's beliefs, society's beliefs, and religion's beliefs.

All our normal tendencies are lost in the process of domestication. And when we are old enough for our mind to understand, we learn the word *no.* The adults say, "Don't do this and don't do that." We rebel and say, "No!" We rebel because we are defending our freedom. We want to be ourselves, but we are very little, and the adults are big and strong. After a certain time we are afraid because we know that every time we do something wrong we are going to be punished.

The domestication is so strong that at a certain point in our life we no longer need anyone to domesticate us. We don't need Mom or Dad, the school or the church to domesticate us. We are so well trained that we are our own domesticator.

We are an autodomesticated animal. We can now domesticate ourselves according to the same belief system we were given, and using the same system of punishment and reward. We punish ourselves when we don't follow the rules according to our belief system; we reward ourselves when we are the "good boy" or "good girl."

The belief system is like a Book of Law that rules our mind. Without question, whatever is in that Book of Law, is our truth. We base all of our judgments according to the Book of Law, even if these judgments go against our own inner nature. Even moral laws like the Ten Commandments are programmed into our mind in the process of domestication. One by one, all these agreements go into the Book of Law, and these agreements rule our dream.

There is something in our minds that judges everybody and everything, including the weather, the dog, the cat — everything. The inner Judge uses what is in our Book of Law to judge everything we do and don't do, everything we think and don't think, and everything we feel and don't feel. Everything lives under the tyranny of this Judge. Every time we do something that goes against the Book of Law, the Judge says we are guilty, we need to be punished, we should be ashamed. This happens many times a day, day after day, for all the years of our lives.

There is another part of us that receives the judgments, and this part is called the Victim. The Victim carries the blame, the guilt, and the shame. It is the part of us that says, "Poor me, I'm not good enough, I'm not intelligent enough, I'm not attractive enough, I'm not worthy of love, poor me." The big Judge agrees and says, "Yes, you are not good enough." And this is all based on a belief system that we never chose to believe. These beliefs are so strong, that even years later when we are exposed to new concepts and try to make our own decisions, we find that these beliefs still control our lives.

Whatever goes against the Book of Law will make you feel a funny sensation in your solar plexus, and it's called fear. Breaking the rules in the Book of Law opens your emotional wounds, and your reaction is to create emotional poison. Because everything that is in the Book of Law has to be true, anything that challenges what you believe is going to make you feel unsafe. Even if the Book of Law is wrong, it makes you *feel safe*.

That is why we need a great deal of courage to challenge our own beliefs. Because even if we know we didn't choose all these beliefs, it is also true that we agreed to all of them. The agreement is so strong that even if we understand the concept of it not being true, we feel the blame, the guilt, and the shame that occur if we go against these rules.

Just as the government has a book of laws that rule the society's dream, our belief system is the Book of Laws that rules our personal dream. All these laws exist in our mind, we believe them, and the Judge inside us bases everything on these rules. The Judge decrees, and the Victim suffers the guilt and punishment. But who says there is justice in this dream? True justice is paying only once for each mistake. True *injustice* is paying more than once for each mistake.

How many times do we pay for one mistake? The answer is thousands of times. The human is the only animal on earth that pays a thousand times for the same mistake. The rest of the animals pay once for every mistake they make. But not us. We have a powerful memory. We make a mistake, we judge ourselves, we find ourselves guilty, and we punish ourselves. If justice exists, then that was enough; we don't need to do it again. But every time we remember, we judge ourselves again, we are guilty again, and we punish ourselves again, and again, and again. If we have a wife or husband he or she also reminds us of the mistake, so we can judge ourselves again, punish ourselves again, and find ourselves guilty again. Is this fair?

How many times do we make our spouse, our children, or our parents pay for the same mistake? Every time we remember the mistake, we blame them again and send them all the emotional poison we feel at the injustice, and then we make them pay again for the same mistake. Is that justice? The Judge in the mind is wrong because the belief system, the Book of Law, is wrong. The whole dream is based on false law. Ninety-five percent of the beliefs we have stored in our minds are nothing but lies, and we suffer because we believe all these lies.

In the dream of the planet it is normal for humans to suffer, to live in fear, and to create emotional dramas. The outside dream is not a pleasant dream; it is a dream of violence, a dream of fear, a dream of war, a dream of injustice. The personal dream of humans will vary, but globally it is mostly a nightmare. If we look at human society we see a place so difficult to live in because it is ruled by fear. Throughout the world we see human suffering, anger, revenge, addictions, violence in the street, and tremendous injustice. It may exist at different levels in different countries around the world, but fear is controlling the outside dream.

If we compare the dream of human society with the description of hell that religions all around the world have promulgated, we find they are exactly the same. Religions say that hell is a place of punishment, a place of fear, pain, and suffering, a place where the fire burns you. Fire is generated by emotions that come from fear. Whenever we feel the emotions of anger, jealousy, envy, or hate, we experience a fire burning within us. We are living in a dream of hell.

If you consider hell as a state of mind, then hell is all around us. Others may warn us that if we don't do what they say we should do, we will go to hell. Bad news! We are already in hell, including the people who tell us that. No human can condemn another to hell because we are already there. Others can put us into a deeper hell, true. But only if we allow this to happen.

Every human has his or her own personal dream, and just like the society dream, it is often ruled by fear. We learn to dream hell in our own life, in our personal dream. The same fears manifest in different ways for each person, of course, but we experience anger, jealousy, hate, envy, and other negative emotions. Our personal dream can also become an ongoing nightmare where we suffer and live in a state of fear. But we don't need to dream a nightmare. It is possible to enjoy a pleasant dream.

All of humanity is searching for truth, justice, and beauty. We are on an eternal search for the truth because we only believe in the lies we have stored in our mind. We are searching for justice because in the belief system we have, there is no justice. We search for beauty because it doesn't matter how beautiful a person is, we don't believe that person has beauty. We keep searching and searching, when everything is already within us. There is no truth to find. Wherever we turn our heads, all we see is the truth, but with the agreements and beliefs we have stored in our mind, we have no eyes for this truth.

We don't see the truth because we are blind. What blinds us are all those false beliefs we have in our mind. We have the need to be right and to make others wrong. We trust what we believe, and our beliefs set us up for suffering. It is as if we live in the middle of a fog that doesn't let us see any further than our own nose. We live in a fog that is not even real. This fog is a dream, your personal dream of life — what you believe, all the concepts you have about what you are, all the agreements you have made with others, with yourself, and even with God.

Your whole mind is a fog which the Toltecs called a *mitote* (pronounced MIH-TOE´-TAY). Your mind is a dream where a thousand people talk at the same time, and nobody understands each other. This is the condition of the human mind — a big *mitote*, and with that big *mitote* you cannot see what you really are. In India they call the *mitote maya*, which means illusion. It is the personality's notion of "I am." Everything you believe about yourself and the world, all the concepts and programming you have in your mind, are all the *mitote*. We cannot see who we truly are; we cannot see that we are not free.

That is why humans resist life. To be alive is the biggest fear humans have. Death is not the biggest fear we have; our biggest fear is taking the risk to be alive — the risk to be alive and express what we really are. Just being ourselves is the biggest fear of humans. We have learned to live our life trying to satisfy other people's demands. We have learned to live by other people's points of view because of the fear of not being accepted and of not being good enough for someone else.

During the process of domestication, we form an image of what perfection is in order to try to be good enough. We create an image of how we should be in order to be accepted by everybody. We especially try to please the ones who love us, like Mom and Dad, big brothers and sisters, the priests and the teacher. Trying to be good enough for them, we create an image of perfection, but we don't fit this image. We create this image, but this image is not real. We are never going to be perfect from this point of view. Never!

Not being perfect, we reject ourselves. And the level of self-rejection depends upon how effective the adults were in breaking our integrity. After domestication it is no longer about being good enough for anybody else. We are not good enough for ourselves because we don't fit with our own image of perfection. We cannot forgive ourselves for not being what we wish to be, or rather what we *believe* we should be. We cannot forgive ourselves for not being perfect.

We know we are not what we believe we are supposed to be and so we feel false, frustrated, and dishonest. We try to hide ourselves, and we pretend to be what we are not. The result is that we feel unauthentic and wear social masks to keep others from noticing this. We are so afraid that somebody else will notice that we are not what we pretend to be. We judge others according to our image of perfection as well, and naturally they fall short of our expectations.

We dishonor ourselves just to please other people. We even do harm to our physical bodies just to be accepted by others. You see teenagers taking drugs just to avoid being rejected by other teenagers. They are not aware that the problem is that they don't accept themselves. They reject themselves because they are not what they pretend to be. They wish to be a certain way, but they are not, and for this they carry shame and guilt. Humans punish themselves endlessly for not being what they believe they should be. They become very self-abusive, and they use other people to abuse themselves as well.

But nobody abuses us more than we abuse ourselves, and it is the Judge, the Victim, and the belief system that make us do this. True, we find people who say their husband or wife, or mother or father, abused them, but you know that we abuse ourselves much more than that. The way we judge ourselves is the worst judge that ever existed. If we make a mistake in front of people, we try to deny the mistake and cover it up. But as soon as we are alone, the Judge becomes so strong, the guilt is so strong, and we feel so stupid, or so bad, or so unworthy.

In your whole life nobody has ever abused you more than you have abused yourself. And the limit of your self-abuse is exactly the limit that you will tolerate from someone else. If someone abuses you a little more than you abuse yourself, you will probably walk away from that person. But if someone abuses you a little less than you abuse yourself, you will probably stay in the relationship and tolerate it endlessly.

If you abuse yourself very badly, you can even tolerate someone who beats you up, humiliates you, and treats you like dirt. Why? Because in your belief system you say, "I deserve it. This person is doing me a favor by being with me. I'm not worthy of love and respect. I'm not good enough."

We have the need to be accepted and to be loved by others, but we cannot accept and love ourselves. The more self-love we have, the less we will experience self-abuse. Self-abuse comes from self-rejection, and self-rejection comes from having an image of what it means to be perfect and never measuring up to that ideal. Our image of perfection is the reason we reject ourselves; it is why we don't accept ourselves the way we are, and why we don't accept others the way they are.

PRELUDE TO A NEW DREAM

There are thousands of agreements you have made with yourself, with other people, with your dream of life, with God, with society, with your parents, with your spouse, with your children. But the most important agreements are the ones you made with yourself. In these agreements you tell yourself who you are, what you feel, what you believe, and how to behave. The result is what you call your personality. In these agreements you say, "This is what I am. This is what I believe. I can do certain things, and some things I cannot do. This is reality, that is fantasy; this is possible, that is impossible."

One single agreement is not such a problem, but we have many agreements that make us suffer, that make us fail in life. If you want to live a life of joy and fulfillment, you have to find the courage to break those agreements that are fear-based and claim your personal power. The agreements that come from fear require us to expend a lot of energy, but the agreements that come from love help us to conserve energy and even gain extra energy.

Each of us is born with a certain amount of personal power that we rebuild every day after we rest. Unfortunately, we spend all our personal power first to create all these agreements and then to keep these agreements. Our personal power is dissipated by all the agreements we have created, and the result is that we feel powerless. We have just enough power to survive each day, because most of it is used to keep the agreements that trap us in the dream of the planet. How can we change the entire dream of our life when we have no power to change even the smallest agreement?

If we can see it is our agreements which rule our life, and we don't like the dream of our life, we need to change the agreements. When we are finally ready to change our agreements, there are four very powerful agreements that will help us break those agreements that come from fear and deplete our energy.

Each time you break an agreement, all the power you used to create it returns to you. If you adopt these four new agreements, they will create enough personal power for you to change the entire system of your old agreements.

You need a very strong will in order to adopt the Four Agreements — but if you can begin to live your life with these agreements, the transformation in your life will be amazing. You will see the drama of hell disappear right before your very eyes. Instead of living in a dream of hell, you will be creating a new dream — your personal dream of heaven.

2

THE FIRST AGREEMENT

Be Impeccable with Your Word

THE FIRST AGREEMENT IS THE MOST IMPORTANT ONE and also the most difficult one to honor. It is so important that with just this first agreement you will be able to transcend to the level of existence I call heaven on earth.

The first agreement is to *be impeccable with your word.* It sounds very simple, but it is very, very powerful.

Why your word? Your word is the power that you have to create. Your word is the gift that comes directly from God. The Gospel of John in the Bible, speaking of the creation of the universe, says, "In the beginning was the word, and the word was with God, and the word is God." Through the word you express your creative power. It is through the word that you manifest everything. Regardless of what language you speak, your intent manifests through the word. What you dream, what you feel, and what you really are, will all be manifested through the word.

The word is not just a sound or a written symbol. The word is a force; it is the power you have to express and communicate, to think, and thereby to create the events in your life. You can speak. What other animal on the planet can speak? The word is the most powerful tool you have as a human; it is the tool of magic. But like a sword with two edges, your word can create the most beautiful dream, or your word can destroy everything around you. One edge is the misuse of the word, which creates a living hell. The other edge is the impeccability of the word, which will only create beauty, love, and heaven on earth. Depending upon how it is used, the word can set you free, or it can enslave you even more than you know. All the magic you possess is based on your word. Your word is pure magic, and misuse of your word is black magic.

The word is so powerful that one word can change a life or destroy the lives of millions of people. Some years ago one man in Germany, by the use of the word, manipulated a whole country of the most intelligent people. He led them into a world war with just the power of his word. He convinced others to commit the most atrocious acts of violence. He activated people's fear with the word, and like a big explosion, there was killing and war all around the world. All over the world humans destroyed other humans because they were afraid of each other. Hitler's word, based on fear-generated beliefs and agreements, will be remembered for centuries.

The human mind is like a fertile ground where seeds are continually being planted. The seeds are opinions, ideas, and concepts. You plant a seed, a thought, and it grows. The word is like a seed, and the human mind is so fertile! The only problem is that too often it is fertile for the seeds of fear. Every human mind is fertile, but only for those kinds of seeds it is prepared for. What is important is to see which kind of seeds our mind is fertile for, and to prepare it to receive the seeds of love.

Take the example of Hitler: He sent out all those seeds of fear, and they grew very strong and beautifully achieved massive destruction. Seeing the awesome power of the word, we must understand what power comes out of our mouths. One fear or doubt planted in our mind can create an endless drama of events. One word is like a spell, and humans use the word like black magicians, thoughtlessly putting spells on each other.

Every human is a magician, and we can either put a spell on someone with our word or we can release someone from a spell. We cast spells all the time with our opinions. An example: I see a friend and give him an opinion that just popped into my mind. I say, "Hmmm! I see that kind of color in your face in people who are going to get cancer." If he listens to the word, and if he agrees, he will have cancer in less than one year. That is the power of the word.

During our domestication, our parents and siblings gave their opinions about us without even thinking. We believed these opinions and we lived in fear over these opinions, like not being good at swimming, or sports, or writing. Someone gives an opinion and says, "Look, this girl is ugly!" The girl listens, believes she is ugly, and grows up with the idea that she is ugly. It doesn't matter how beautiful she is; as long as she has that agreement, she will believe that she is ugly. That is the spell she is under.

By hooking our attention, the word can enter our mind and change a whole belief for better or for worse. Another example: You may believe you are stupid, and you may have believed this for as long as you can remember. This agreement can be very tricky, causing you to do a lot of things just to ensure that you are stupid. You may do something and think to yourself, "I wish I were smart, but I must be stupid or I wouldn't have done that." The mind goes in hundreds of different directions, and we could spend days getting hooked by just that one belief in our own stupidity.

Then one day someone hooks your attention and using the word, lets you know that you are not stupid. You believe what the person says and make a new agreement. As a result, you no longer feel or act stupid. A whole spell is broken, just by the power of the word. Conversely, if you believe you are stupid, and someone hooks your attention and says, "Yes, you are really the most stupid person I have ever met," the agreement will be reinforced and become even stronger.

Now let us see what the word *impeccability* means. *Impeccability* means "without sin." *Impeccable* comes from the Latin *pecatus,* which means "sin." The *im* in impeccable means "without," so *impeccable* means "without sin." Religions talk about sin and sinners, but let's understand what it really means to sin. A sin is anything that you do which goes against yourself. Everything you feel or believe or say that goes against yourself is a sin. You go against yourself when you judge or blame yourself for anything. Being without sin is exactly the opposite. Being impeccable is not going against yourself. When you are impeccable, you take responsibility for your actions, but you do not judge or blame yourself.

From this point of view, the whole concept of sin changes from something moral or religious to something commonsense. Sin begins with rejection of yourself. Self-rejection is the biggest sin that you commit. In religious terms self-rejection is a "mortal sin," which leads to death. Impeccability, on the other hand, leads to life.

Being impeccable with your word is not using the word against yourself. If I see you in the street and I call you stupid, it appears that I'm using the word against you. But really I'm using my word against myself, because you're going to hate me for this, and your hating me is not good for me. Therefore, if I get angry and with my word send all that emotional poison to you, I'm using the word against myself.

If I love myself I will express that love in my interactions with you, and then I am being impeccable with the word, because that action will produce a like reaction. If I love you, then you will love me. If I insult you, you will insult me. If I have gratitude for you, you will have gratitude for me. If I'm selfish with you, you will be selfish with me. If I use the word to put a spell on you, you are going to put a spell on me.

Being impeccable with your word is the correct use of your energy; it means to use your energy in the direction of truth and love for yourself. If you make an agreement with yourself to be impeccable with your word, just with that intention, the truth will manifest through you and clean all the emotional poison that exists within you. But making this agreement is difficult because we have learned to do precisely the opposite. We have learned to lie as a habit of our communication with others and more importantly with ourselves. We are not impeccable with the word.

The power of the word is completely misused in hell. We use the word to curse, to blame, to find guilt, to destroy. Of course, we also use it in the right way, but not too often. Mostly we use the word to spread our personal poison — to express anger, jealousy, envy, and hate. The word is pure magic — the most powerful gift we have as humans — and we use it against ourselves. We plan revenge. We create chaos with the word. We use the word to create hate between different races, between different people, between families, between nations. We misuse the word so often, and this misuse is how we create and perpetuate the dream of hell. Misuse of the word is how we pull each other down and keep each other in a state of fear and doubt. Because the word is the magic that humans possess and misuse of the word is black magic, we are using black magic all the time without knowing that our word is magic at all.

There was a woman, for example, who was intelligent and had a very good heart. She had a daughter whom she adored and loved very much. One night she came home from a very bad day at work, tired, full of emotional tension, and with a terrible headache. She wanted peace and quiet, but her daughter was singing and jumping happily. The daughter was unaware of how her mother was feeling; she was in her own world, in her own dream. She felt so wonderful, and she was jumping and singing louder and louder, expressing her joy and her love. She was singing so loud that it made her mother's headache even worse, and at a certain moment, the mother lost control. Angrily she looked at her beautiful little girl and said, "Shut up! You have an ugly voice. Can you just shut up!"

The truth is that the mother's tolerance for any noise was nonexistent; it was not that the little girl's voice was ugly. But the daughter believed what her mother said, and in that moment she made an agreement with herself. After that she no longer sang, because she believed her voice was ugly and would bother anyone who heard it. She became shy at school, and if she was asked to sing, she refused. Even speaking to others became difficult for her. Everything changed in the little girl because of this new agreement: She believed she must repress her emotions in order to be accepted and loved.

Whenever we hear an opinion and believe it, we make an agreement, and it becomes part of our belief system. This little girl grew up, and even though she had a beautiful voice, she never sang again. She developed a whole complex from one spell. This spell was cast upon her by the one who loved her the most: her own mother. Her mother didn't notice what she did with her word. She didn't notice that she used black magic and put a spell on her daughter. She didn't know the power of her word, and therefore she isn't to blame. She did what her own mother, father, and others had done to her in many ways. They misused the word.

How many times do we do this with our own children? We give them these types of opinions and our children carry that black magic for years and years. People who love us do black magic on us, but they don't know what they do. That is why we must forgive them; they don't know what they do.

Another example: You awake in the morning feeling very happy. You feel so wonderful, you stay one or two hours in front of the mirror, making yourself beautiful. Well, one of your best friends says, "What has happened to you? You look so ugly. Look at the dress you are wearing; you look ridiculous." That's it; that is enough to put you all the way down in hell. Maybe this girlfriend just told you this to hurt you. And, she did. She gave you an opinion with all the power of her word behind it. If you accept the opinion, it becomes an agreement now, and you put all your power into that opinion. That opinion becomes black magic.

These types of spells are difficult to break. The only thing that can break a spell is to make a new agreement based on truth. The truth is the most important part of being impeccable with your word. On one side of the sword are the lies which create black magic, and on the other side of the sword is the truth which has the power to break the spell of black magic. Only the truth will set us free.

❧

Looking at everyday human interactions, imagine how many times we cast spells on each other with our word. Over time this interaction has become the worst form of black magic, and we call it *gossip.*

Gossip is black magic at its very worst because it is pure poison. We learned how to gossip by agreement. When we were children, we heard the adults around us gossiping all the time, openly giving their opinions about other people. They even had opinions about people they didn't know. Emotional poison was transferred along with the opinions, and we learned this as the normal way to communicate.

Gossiping has become the main form of communication in human society. It has become the way we feel close to each other, because it makes us feel better to see someone else feel as badly as we do. There is an old expression that says, "Misery likes company," and people who are suffering in hell don't want to be all alone. Fear and suffering are an important part of the dream of the planet; they are how the dream of the planet keeps us down.

Using the analogy of the human mind as a computer, gossip can be compared to a computer virus. A computer virus is a piece of computer language written in the same language all the other codes are written in, but with a harmful intent. This code is inserted into the program of your computer when you least expect it and most of the time without your awareness. After this code has been introduced, your computer doesn't work quite right, or it doesn't function at all because the codes get so mixed up with so many conflicting messages that it stops producing good results.

Human gossip works exactly the same way. For example, you are beginning a new class with a new teacher and you have looked forward to it for a long time. On the first day of class, you run into someone who took the class before, who tells you, "Oh that instructor was such a pompous jerk! He didn't know what he was talking about, and he was a pervert too, so watch out!"

You are immediately imprinted with the word and the emotional code the person had when saying this, but what you are not aware of is his or her motivation in telling you. This person could be angry for failing the class or simply making an assumption based on fears and prejudices, but because you have learned to ingest information like a child, some part of you believes the gossip, and you go on to the class.

As the teacher speaks, you feel the poison come up inside you and you don't realize you see the teacher through the eyes of the person who gave you that gossip. Then you start talking to other people in the class about this, and they start to see the teacher in the same way: as a jerk and a pervert. You really hate the class, and soon you decide to drop out. You blame the teacher, but it is gossip that is to blame.

All of this mess can be caused by one little computer virus. One little piece of misinformation can break down communication between people, causing every person it touches to become infected and contagious to others. Imagine that every single time others gossip to you, they insert a computer virus into your mind, causing you to think a little less clearly every time. Then imagine that in an effort to clean up your own confusion and get some relief from the poison, you gossip and spread these viruses to someone else.

Now imagine this pattern going on in a never-ending chain between all the humans on earth. The result is a world full of humans who can only read information through circuits that are clogged with a poisonous, contagious virus. Once again, this poisonous virus is what the Toltecs called the *mitote*, the chaos of a thousand different voices all trying to talk at once in the mind.

Even worse are the black magicians or "computer hackers" who intentionally spread the virus. Think back to a time when you or someone you know was angry with someone else and desired revenge. In order to seek revenge you said something to or about that person with the intention of spreading poison and making that person feel bad about him- or herself. As children we do this quite thoughtlessly, but as we grow older we become much more calculated in our efforts to bring other people down. Then we lie to ourselves and say that person received a just punishment for their wrongdoing.

When we see the world through a computer virus, it is easy to justify the cruelest behavior. What we don't see is that misuse of our word is putting us deeper into hell.

~

For years we have received the gossip and spells from the words of others, but also from the way we use our word with ourselves. We talk to ourselves constantly and most of the time we say things like, "Oh, I look fat, I look ugly. I'm getting old, I'm losing my hair. I'm stupid, I never understand anything. I will never be good enough, and I'm never going to be perfect." Do you see how we use the word against ourselves? We must begin to understand what the word *is* and what the word *does*. If you understand the first agreement, *be impeccable with your word*, you begin to see all the changes that can happen in your life. Changes first in the way you deal with yourself, and later in the way you deal with other people, especially those you love the most.

Consider how many times you have gossiped about the person you love the most to gain the support of others for your point of view. How many times have you hooked other people's attention, and spread poison about your loved one in order to make your opinion right? Your opinion is nothing but your point of view. It is not necessarily true. Your opinion comes from your beliefs, your own ego, and your own dream. We create all this poison and spread it to others just so we can feel right about our own point of view.

If we adopt the first agreement, and become impeccable with our word, any emotional poison will eventually be cleaned from our mind and from our communication in our personal relationships, including with our pet dog or cat.

Impeccability of the word will also give you immunity from anyone putting a negative spell on you. You will only receive a negative idea if your mind is fertile ground for that idea. When you become impeccable with your word, your mind is no longer fertile ground for words that come from black magic. Instead, it is fertile for the words that come from love. You can measure the impeccability of your word by your level of self-love. How much you love yourself and how you feel about yourself are directly proportionate to the quality and integrity of your word. When you are impeccable with your word, you feel good; you feel happy and at peace.

You can transcend the dream of hell just by making the agreement to be impeccable with your word. Right now I am planting that seed in your mind. Whether or not the seed grows depends upon how fertile your mind is for the seeds of love. It is up to you to make this agreement with yourself: *I am impeccable with my word.* Nurture this seed, and as it grows in your mind, it will generate more seeds of love to replace the seeds of fear. This first agreement will change the kind of seeds your mind is fertile for.

Be impeccable with your word. This is the first agreement that you should make if you want to be free, if you want to be happy, if you want to transcend the level of existence that is hell. It is very powerful. Use the word in the correct way. Use the word to share your love. Use white magic, beginning with yourself. Tell yourself how wonderful you are, how great you are. Tell yourself how much you love yourself. Use the word to break all those teeny, tiny agreements that make you suffer.

It is possible. It is possible because I did it, and I am no better than you. No, we are exactly the same. We have the same kind of brain, the same kind of bodies; we are humans. If I was able to break those agreements and create new agreements, then you can do the same. If I can be impeccable with my word, why not you? Just this one agreement can change your whole life. Impeccability of the word can lead you to personal freedom, to huge success and abundance; it can take away all fear and transform it into joy and love.

Just imagine what you can create with impeccability of the word. With the impeccability of the word you can transcend the dream of fear and live a different life. You can live in heaven in the middle of thousands of people living in hell because you are immune to that hell. You can attain the kingdom of heaven from this one agreement: *Be impeccable with your word.*

3

THE SECOND AGREEMENT

Don't Take Anything Personally

THE NEXT THREE AGREEMENTS ARE REALLY BORN from the first agreement. The second agreement is *don't take anything personally.*

Whatever happens around you, don't take it personally. Using an earlier example, if I see you on the street and I say, "Hey, you are so stupid," without knowing you, it's not about you; it's about me. If you take it personally, then perhaps you believe you are stupid. Maybe you think to yourself, "How does he know? Is he clairvoyant, or can everybody see how stupid I am?"

You take it personally because you agree with whatever was said. As soon as you agree, the poison goes through you, and you are trapped in the dream of hell. What causes you to be trapped is what we call *personal importance.* Personal importance, or taking things personally, is the maximum expression of selfishness because we make the assumption that everything is about "me." During the period of our education, or our domestication, we learn to take everything personally. We think we are responsible for everything. Me, me, me, always me!

Nothing other people do is because of you. It is because of themselves. All people live in their own dream, in their own mind; they are in a completely different world from the one we live in. When we take something personally, we make the assumption that they know what is in our world, and we try to impose our world on their world.

Even when a situation seems so personal, even if others insult you directly, it has nothing to do with you. What they say, what they do, and the opinions they give are according to the agreements they have in their own minds. Their point of view comes from all the programming they received during domestication.

If someone gives you an opinion and says, "Hey, you look so fat," don't take it personally, because the truth is that this person is dealing with his or her own feelings, beliefs, and opinions. That person tried to send poison to you and if you take it personally, then you take that poison and it becomes yours. Taking things personally makes you easy prey for these predators, the black magicians. They can hook you easily with one little opinion and feed you whatever poison they want, and because you take it personally, you eat it up.

You eat all their emotional garbage, and now it becomes your garbage. But if you do not take it personally, you are immune in the middle of hell.

Immunity to poison in the middle of hell is the gift of this agreement.

When you take things personally, then you feel offended, and your reaction is to defend your beliefs and create conflicts. You make something big out of something so little, because you have the need to be right and make everybody else wrong. You also try hard to be right by giving them your own opinions. In the same way, whatever you feel and do is just a projection of your own personal dream, a reflection of your own agreements. What you say, what you do, and the opinions you have are according to the agreements you have made — and these opinions have nothing to do with me.

It is not important to me what you think about me, and I don't take what you think personally. I don't take it personally when people say, "Miguel, you are the best," and I also don't take it personally when they say, "Miguel, you are the worst." I know that when you are happy you will tell me, "Miguel, you are such an angel!" But, when you are mad at me you will say, "Oh, Miguel, you are such a devil! You are so disgusting. How can you say those things?" Either way, it does not affect me because I know what I am. I don't have the need to be accepted. I don't have the need to have someone tell me, "Miguel, you are doing so good!" or "How dare you do that!"

No, I don't take it personally. Whatever you think, whatever you feel, I know is your problem and not my problem. It is the way you see the world. It is nothing personal, because you are dealing with yourself, not with me. Others are going to have their own opinion according to their belief system, so nothing they think about me is really about me, but it is about them.

You may even tell me, "Miguel, what you are saying is hurting me." But it is not what I am saying that is hurting you; it is that you have wounds that I touch by what I have said. You are hurting yourself. There is no way that I can take this personally. Not because I don't believe in you or don't trust you, but because I know that you see the world with different eyes, with your eyes. You create an entire picture or movie in your mind, and in that picture you are the director, you are the producer, you are the main actor or actress. Everyone else is a secondary actor or actress. It is your movie.

The way you see that movie is according to the agreements you have made with life. Your point of view is something personal to you. It is no one's truth but yours. Then, if you get mad at me, I know you are dealing with yourself. I am the excuse for you to get mad. And you get mad because you are afraid, because you are dealing with fear. If you are not afraid, there is no way you will get mad at me. If you are not afraid, there is no way you will hate me. If you are not afraid, there is no way you will be jealous or sad.

If you live without fear, if you love, there is no place for any of those emotions. If you don't feel any of those emotions, it is logical that you will feel good. When you feel good, everything around you is good. When everything around you is great, everything makes you happy. You are loving everything that is around you, because you are loving yourself. Because you like the way you are. Because you are content with you. Because you are happy with your life. You are happy with the movie that you are producing, happy with your agreements with life. You are at peace, and you are happy. You live in that state of bliss where everything is so wonderful, and everything is so beautiful. In that state of bliss you are making love all the time with everything that you perceive.

&

Whatever people do, feel, think, or say, *don't take it personally*. If they tell you how wonderful you are, they are not saying that because of you. You know you are wonderful. It is not necessary to believe other people who tell you that you are wonderful. Don't take *anything* personally. Even if someone got a gun and shot you in the head, it was nothing personal. Even at that extreme.

Even the opinions you have about yourself are not necessarily true; therefore, you don't need to take whatever you hear in your own mind personally. The mind has the ability to talk to itself, but it also has the ability to hear information that is available from other realms. Sometimes you hear a voice in your mind, and you may wonder where it came from. This voice may have come from another reality in which there are living beings very similar to the human mind. The Toltecs called these beings Allies. In Europe, Africa, and India they called them the Gods.

Our mind also exists in the level of the Gods. Our mind also lives in that reality and can perceive that reality. The mind sees with the eyes and perceives this waking reality. But the mind also sees and perceives without the eyes, although the reason is hardly aware of this perception. The mind lives in more than one dimension. There may be times when you have ideas that don't originate in your mind, but you are perceiving them with your mind. You have the right to believe or not believe these voices and the right not to take what they say personally. We have a choice whether or not to believe the voices we hear within our own minds, just as we have a choice of what to believe and agree with in the dream of the planet.

The mind can also talk and listen to itself. The mind is divided as your body is divided. Just as you can say, "I have one hand, and I can shake my other hand and feel the other hand," the mind can talk to itself. Part of the mind is speaking, and the other part is listening. It is a big problem when a thousand parts of your mind are all speaking at the same time. This is called a *mitote*, remember?

The *mitote* can be compared to a huge marketplace where thousands of people are talking and bartering at the same time. Each one has different thoughts and feelings; each one has a different point of view. The programming in the mind — all of those agreements we have made — are not necessarily compatible with each other. Every agreement is like a separate living being; it has its own personality and its own voice. There are conflicting agreements that go against other agreements and on and on until it becomes a big war in the mind. The *mitote* is the reason humans hardly know what they want, how they want it, or when they want it. They don't agree with themselves because there are parts of the mind that want one thing, and other parts that want exactly the opposite.

Some part of the mind has objections to certain thoughts and actions, and another part supports the actions of the opposing thoughts. All these little living beings create inner conflict because they are alive and they each have a voice. Only by making an inventory of our agreements will we uncover all of the conflicts in the mind and eventually make order out of the chaos of the *mitote*.

❧

Don't take anything personally because by taking things personally you set yourself up to suffer for nothing. Humans are addicted to suffering at different levels and to different degrees, and we support each other in maintaining these addictions. Humans agree to help each other suffer. If you have the need to be abused, you will find it easy to be abused by others. Likewise, if you are with people who need to suffer, something in you makes you abuse them. It is as if they have a note on their back that says, "Please kick me." They are asking for justification for their suffering. Their addiction to suffering is nothing but an agreement that is reinforced every day.

Wherever you go you will find people lying to you, and as your awareness grows, you will notice that you also lie to yourself. Do not expect people to tell you the truth because they also lie to themselves. You have to trust yourself and choose to believe or not to believe what someone says to you.

When we really see other people as they are without taking it personally, we can never be hurt by what they say or do. Even if others lie to you, it is okay. They are lying to you because they are afraid. They are afraid you will discover that they are not perfect. It is painful to take that social mask off. If others say one thing, but do another, you are lying to yourself if you don't listen to their actions. But if you are truthful with yourself, you will save yourself a lot of emotional pain. Telling yourself the truth about it may hurt, but you don't need to be attached to the pain. Healing is on the way, and it's just a matter of time before things will be better for you.

If someone is not treating you with love and respect, it is a gift if they walk away from you. If that person doesn't walk away, you will surely endure many years of suffering with him or her. Walking away may hurt for a while, but your heart will eventually heal. Then you can choose what you really want. You will find that you don't need to trust others as much as you need to trust yourself to make the right choices.

When you make it a strong habit not to take anything personally, you avoid many upsets in your life. Your anger, jealousy, and envy will disappear, and even your sadness will simply disappear if you don't take things personally.

If you can make this second agreement a habit, you will find that nothing can put you back into hell. There is a huge amount of freedom that comes to you when you take nothing personally. You become immune to black magicians, and no spell can affect you regardless of how strong it may be. The whole world can gossip about you, and if you don't take it personally you are immune. Someone can intentionally send emotional poison, and if you don't take it personally, you will not eat it. When you don't take the emotional poison, it becomes even worse in the sender, but not in you.

You can see how important this agreement is. Taking nothing personally helps you to break many habits and routines that trap you in the dream of hell and cause needless suffering. Just by practicing this second agreement you begin to break dozens of teeny, tiny agreements that cause you to suffer. And if you practice the first two agreements, you will break seventy-five percent of the teeny, tiny agreements that keep you trapped in hell.

Write this agreement on paper, and put it on your refrigerator to remind you all the time: *Don't take anything personally.*

As you make a habit of not taking anything personally, you won't need to place your trust in what others do or say. You will only need to trust yourself to make responsible choices. You are never responsible for the actions of others; you are only responsible for you. When you truly understand this, and refuse to take things personally, you can hardly be hurt by the careless comments or actions of others.

If you keep this agreement, you can travel around the world with your heart completely open and no one can hurt you. You can say, "I love you," without fear of being ridiculed or rejected. You can ask for what you need. You can say yes, or you can say no — whatever you choose — without guilt or self-judgment. You can choose to follow your heart always. Then you can be in the middle of hell and still experience inner peace and happiness. You can stay in your state of bliss, and hell will not affect you at all.

4

THE THIRD AGREEMENT

Don't Make Assumptions

THE THIRD AGREEMENT IS *DON'T MAKE ASSUMPTIONS.*

We have the tendency to make assumptions about everything. The problem with making assumptions is that we *believe* they are the truth. We could swear they are real. We make assumptions about what others are doing or thinking — we take it personally — then we blame them and react by sending emotional poison with our word. That is why whenever we make assumptions, we're asking for problems. We make an assumption, we misunderstand, we take it personally, and we end up creating a whole big drama for nothing.

All the sadness and drama you have lived in your life was rooted in making assumptions and taking things personally. Take a moment to consider the truth of this statement. The whole world of control between humans is about making assumptions and taking things personally. Our whole dream of hell is based on that.

We create a lot of emotional poison just by making assumptions and taking it personally, because usually we start gossiping about our assumptions. Remember, gossiping is the way we communicate to each other in the dream of hell and transfer poison to one another. Because we are afraid to ask for clarification, we make assumptions, and believe we are right about the assumptions; then we defend our assumptions and try to make someone else wrong.

It is always better to ask questions than to make an assumption, because assumptions set us up for suffering.

The big *mitote* in the human mind creates a lot of chaos which causes us to misinterpret everything and misunderstand everything. We only see what we want to see and hear what we want to hear. We don't perceive things the way they are. We have the habit of dreaming with no basis in reality. We literally dream things up in our imaginations. Because we don't understand something, we make an assumption about the meaning, and when the truth comes out, the bubble of our dream pops and we find out it was not what we thought it was at all.

An example: You are walking in the mall, and you see a person you like. That person turns to you and smiles, and then walks away. You can make a lot of assumptions just because of this one experience. With these assumptions you can create a whole fantasy. And you really want to believe this fantasy and make it real. A whole dream begins to form just from your assumptions, and you can believe, "Oh, this person really likes me." In your mind a whole relationship begins from that. Maybe you even get married in this fantasyland. But the fantasy is in *your* mind, in your personal dream.

Making assumptions in our relationships is really asking for problems. Often we make the assumption that our partners know what we think and that we don't have to say what we want. We assume they are going to do what we want, because they know us so well. If they don't do what we assume they should do, we feel so hurt and say, "You should have known."

Another example: You decide to get married, and you make the assumption that your partner sees marriage the same way that you do. Then you live together and you find out this is not true. This creates a lot of conflict, but you still don't try to clarify your feelings about marriage. The husband comes home from work and the wife is mad, and the husband doesn't know why. Maybe it's because the wife made an assumption. Without telling him what she wants, she makes an assumption that he knows her so well, that he knows what she wants, as if he can read her mind. She gets so upset because he fails to meet her expectations. Making assumptions in relationships leads to a lot of fights, a lot of difficulties, a lot of misunderstandings with people we supposedly love.

In any kind of relationship we can make the assumption that others know what we think, and we don't have to say what we want. They are going to do what we want because they know us so well. If they don't do what we want, what we assume they should do, we feel hurt and think, "How could you do that? You should know." Again, we make the assumption that the other person knows what we want. A whole drama is created because we make this assumption and then put more assumptions on top of it.

It is very interesting how the human mind works. We have the need to justify everything, to explain and understand everything, in order to feel safe. We have millions of questions that need answers because there are so many things that the reasoning mind cannot explain. It is not important if the answer is correct; just the answer itself makes us feel safe. This is why we make assumptions.

If others tell us something, we make assumptions, and if they don't tell us something we make assumptions to fulfill our need to know and to replace the need to communicate. Even if we hear something and we don't understand, we make assumptions about what it means and then believe the assumptions. We make all sorts of assumptions because we don't have the courage to ask questions.

These assumptions are made so fast and unconsciously most of the time because we have agreements to communicate this way. We have agreed that it is not safe to ask questions; we have agreed that if people love us, they should know what we want or how we feel. When we believe something, we assume we are right about it to the point that we will destroy relationships in order to defend our position.

We make the assumption that everyone sees life the way *we* do. We assume that others think the way we think, feel the way we feel, judge the way we judge, and abuse the way we abuse. This is the biggest assumption that humans make. And this is why we have a fear of being ourselves around others. Because we think everyone else will judge us, victimize us, abuse us, and blame us as we do ourselves. So even before others have a chance to reject us, we have already rejected ourselves. That is the way the human mind works.

We also make assumptions about ourselves, and this creates a lot of inner conflict. "I think I am able to do this." You make this assumption, for instance, then you discover you aren't able to do it. You overestimate or underestimate yourself because you haven't taken the time to ask yourself questions and to answer them. Perhaps you need to gather more facts about a particular situation. Or maybe you need to stop lying to yourself about what you truly want.

Often when you go into a relationship with someone you like, you have to justify why you like that person. You only see what you want to see and you deny there are things you don't like about that person. You lie to yourself just to make yourself right. Then you make assumptions, and one of the assumptions is "My love will change this person." But this is not true. Your love will not change anybody. If others change, it's because they want to change, not because you can change them. Then something happens between the two of you, and you get hurt. Suddenly you see what you didn't want to see before, only now it is amplified by your emotional poison. Now you have to justify your emotional pain and blame them for your choices.

We don't need to justify love; it is there or not there. Real love is accepting other people the way they are without trying to change them. If we try to change them, this means we don't really like them. Of course, if you decide to live with someone, if you make that agreement, it is always better to make that agreement with someone who is exactly the way you want him or her to be. Find someone whom you don't have to change at all. It is much easier to find someone who is already the way you want him or her to be, instead of trying to change that person. Also, that person must love you just the way you are, so he or she doesn't have to change you at all. If others feel they have to change you, that means they really don't love you just the way you are. So why be with someone if you're not the way he or she wants you to be?

We have to be what we are, so we don't have to present a false image. If you love me the way I am, "Okay, take me." If you don't love me the way I am, "Okay, bye-bye. Find someone else." It may sound harsh, but this kind of communication means the personal agreements we make with others are clear and impeccable.

Just imagine the day that you stop making assumptions with your partner and eventually with everyone else in your life. Your way of communicating will change completely, and your relationships will no longer suffer from conflicts created by mistaken assumptions.

The way to keep yourself from making assumptions is to ask questions. Make sure the communication is clear. If you don't understand, ask. Have the courage to ask questions until you are clear as you can be, and even then do not assume you know all there is to know about a given situation. Once you hear the answer, you will not have to make assumptions because you will know the truth.

Also, find your voice to ask for what you want. Everybody has the right to tell you no or yes, but you always have the right to ask. Likewise, everybody has the right to ask you, and you have the right to say yes or no.

If you don't understand something, it is better for you to ask and be clear, instead of making an assumption. The day you stop making assumptions you will communicate cleanly and clearly, free of emotional poison. Without making assumptions your word becomes impeccable.

With clear communication, all of your relationships will change, not only with your partner, but with everyone else. You won't need to make assumptions because everything becomes so clear. This is what I want; this is what you want. If we communicate in this way, our word becomes impeccable. If all humans could communicate in this way, with impeccability of the word, there would be no wars, no violence, no misunderstandings. All human problems would be resolved if we could just have good, clear communication.

This, then, is the Third Agreement: *Don't make assumptions.* Just saying this sounds easy, but I understand that it is difficult to do. It is difficult because we so often do exactly the opposite. We have all these habits and routines that we are not even aware of. Becoming aware of these habits and understanding the importance of this agreement is the first step. But understanding its importance is not enough. Information or an idea is merely the seed in your mind. What will really make the difference is action.

Taking the action over and over again strengthens your will, nurtures the seed, and establishes a solid foundation for the new habit to grow. After many repetitions these new agreements will become second nature, and you will see how the magic of your word transforms you from a black magician into a white magician.

A white magician uses the word for creation, giving, sharing, and loving. By making this one agreement a habit, your whole life will be completely transformed.

When you transform your whole dream, magic just happens in your life. What you need comes to you easily because spirit moves freely through you. This is the mastery of intent, the mastery of the spirit, the mastery of love, the mastery of gratitude, and the mastery of life. This is the goal of the Toltec. This is the path to personal freedom.

5

THE FOURTH AGREEMENT

Always Do Your Best

THERE IS JUST ONE MORE AGREEMENT, BUT IT'S THE one that allows the other three to become deeply ingrained habits. The fourth agreement is about the action of the first three: *Always do your best.*

Under any circumstance, always do your best, no more and no less. But keep in mind that your best is never going to be the same from one moment to the next. Everything is alive and changing all the time, so your best will sometimes be high quality, and other times it will not be as good. When you wake up refreshed and energized in the morning, your best will be better than when you are tired at night. Your best will be different when you are healthy as opposed to sick, or sober as opposed to drunk. Your best will depend on whether you are feeling wonderful and happy, or upset, angry, or jealous.

In your everyday moods your best can change from one moment to another, from one hour to the next, from one day to another. Your best will also change over time. As you build the habit of the four new agreements, your best will become better than it used to be.

Regardless of the quality, keep doing your best — no more and no less than your best. If you try too hard to do more than your best, you will spend more energy than is needed and in the end your best will not be enough. When you overdo, you deplete your body and go against yourself, and it will take you longer to accomplish your goal. But if you do less than your best, you subject yourself to frustrations, self-judgment, guilt, and regrets.

Just do your best — in any circumstance in your life. It doesn't matter if you are sick or tired, if you always do your best there is no way you can judge yourself. And if you don't judge yourself there is no way you are going to suffer from guilt, blame, and self-punishment. By always doing your best, you will break a big spell that you have been under.

There was a man who wanted to transcend his suffering so he went to a Buddhist temple to find a Master to help him. He went to the Master and asked, "Master, if I meditate four hours a day, how long will it take me to transcend?"

The Master looked at him and said, "If you meditate four hours a day, perhaps you will transcend in ten years."

Thinking he could do better, the man then said, "Oh, Master, what if I meditated eight hours a day, how long will it take me to transcend?"

The Master looked at him and said, "If you meditate eight hours a day, perhaps you will transcend in twenty years."

"But why will it take me longer if I meditate more?" the man asked.

The Master replied, "You are not here to sacrifice your joy or your life. You are here to live, to be happy, and to love. If you can do your best in two hours of meditation, but you spend eight hours instead, you will only grow tired, miss the point, and you won't enjoy your life. Do your best, and perhaps you will learn that no matter how long you meditate, you can live, love, and be happy."

❧

Doing your best, you are going to live your life intensely. You are going to be productive, you are going to be good to yourself, because you will be giving yourself to your family, to your community, to everything. But it is the action that is going to make you feel intensely happy. When you always do your best, you take action. Doing your best is taking the action because you love it, not because you're expecting a reward. Most people do exactly the opposite: They only take action when they expect a reward, and they don't enjoy the action. And that's the reason why they don't do their best.

For example, most people go to work every day just thinking of payday, and the money they will get from the work they are doing. They can hardly wait for Friday or Saturday, whatever day they receive their money and can take time off. They are working for the reward, and as a result they resist work. They try to avoid the action and it becomes more difficult, and they don't do their best.

They work so hard all week long, suffering the work, suffering the action, not because they like to, but because they feel they have to. They have to work because they have to pay the rent, because they have to support their family. They have all that frustration, and when they do receive their money they are unhappy. They have two days to rest, to do what they want to do, and what do they do? They try to escape. They get drunk because they don't like themselves. They don't like their life. There are many ways that we hurt ourselves when we don't like who we are.

On the other hand, if you take action just for the sake of doing it, without expecting a reward, you will find that you enjoy every action you do. Rewards will come, but you are not attached to the reward. You can even get more than you would have imagined for yourself without expecting a reward. If we like what we do, if we always do our best, then we are really enjoying life. We are having fun, we don't get bored, we don't have frustrations.

When you do your best, you don't give the Judge the opportunity to find you guilty or to blame you. If you have done your best and the Judge tries to judge you according to your Book of Laws, you've got the answer: "I did my best." There are no regrets. That is why we always do our best. It is not an easy agreement to keep, but this agreement is really going to set you free.

When you do your best you learn to accept yourself. But you have to be aware and learn from your mistakes. Learning from your mistakes means you practice, look honestly at the results, and keep practicing. This increases your awareness.

Doing your best really doesn't feel like work because you enjoy whatever you are doing. You know you're doing your best when you are enjoying the action or doing it in a way that will not have negative repercussions for you. You do your best because you want to do it, not because you have to do it, not because you are trying to please the Judge, and not because you are trying to please other people.

If you take action because you have to, then there is no way you are going to do your best. Then it is better not to do it. No, you do your best because doing your best all the time makes *you* so happy. When you are doing your best just for the pleasure of doing it, you are taking action because you enjoy the action.

Action is about living fully. Inaction is the way that we deny life. Inaction is sitting in front of the television every day for years because you are afraid to be alive and to take the risk of expressing what you are. Expressing what you are is taking action. You can have many great ideas in your head, but what makes the difference is the action. Without action upon an idea, there will be no manifestation, no results, and no reward.

A good example of this comes from the story about Forrest Gump. He didn't have great ideas, but he took action. He was happy because he always did his best at whatever he did. He was richly rewarded without expecting any reward at all. Taking action is being alive. It's taking the risk to go out and express your dream. This is different than imposing your dream on someone else, because everyone has the right to express his or her dream.

Doing your best is a great habit to have. I do my best in everything I do and feel. Doing my best has become a ritual in my life because I made the choice to make it a ritual. It's a belief like any other belief that I choose. I make everything a ritual, and I always do my best. Taking a shower is a ritual for me, and with that action I tell my body how much I love it. I feel and enjoy the water on my body. I do my best to fulfill the needs of my body. I do my best to give to my body and to receive what my body gives to me.

In India they perform a ritual called *puja*. In this ritual, they take idols that represent God in many different forms and bathe them, feed them, and give their love to them. They even chant mantras to these idols. The idol itself is not important. What is important is the way they perform the ritual, the way they say, "I love you, God."

God is life. God is life in action. The best way to say, "I love you, God," is to live your life doing your best. The best way to say, "Thank you, God," is by letting go of the past and living in the present moment, right here and now. Whatever life takes away from you, let it go. When you surrender and let go of the past, you allow yourself to be fully alive in the moment. Letting go of the past means you can enjoy the dream that is happening right now.

If you live in a past dream, you don't enjoy what is happening right now because you will always wish it to be different than it is. There is no time to miss anyone or anything because you are alive. Not enjoying what is happening right now is living in the past and being only half alive. This leads to self-pity, suffering, and tears.

You were born with the right to be happy. You were born with the right to love, to enjoy and to share your love. You are alive, so take your life and enjoy it. Don't resist life passing through you, because that is God passing through you. Just your existence proves the existence of God. Your existence proves the existence of life and energy.

We don't need to know or prove anything. Just to be, to take a risk and enjoy your life, is all that matters. Say no when you want to say no, and yes when you want to say yes. You have the right to be you. You can only be you when you do your best. When you don't do your best you are denying yourself the right to be you. That's a seed that you should really nurture in your mind. You don't need knowledge or great philosophical concepts. You don't need the acceptance of others. You express your own divinity by being alive and by loving yourself and others. It is an expression of God to say, "Hey, I love you."

The first three agreements will only work if you do your best. Don't expect that you will always be able to be impeccable with your word. Your routine habits are too strong and firmly rooted in your mind. But you can do your best. Don't expect that you will never take anything personally; just do your best. Don't expect that you will never make another assumption, but you can certainly do your best.

By doing your best, the habits of misusing your word, taking things personally, and making assumptions will become weaker and less frequent with time. You don't need to judge yourself, feel guilty, or punish yourself if you cannot keep these agreements. If you're doing your best, you will feel good about yourself even if you still make assumptions, still take things personally, and still are not impeccable with your word.

If you do your best always, over and over again, you will become a master of transformation. Practice makes the master. By doing your best *you* become a master. Everything you have ever learned, you learned through repetition. You learned to write, to drive, and even to walk by repetition. You are a master of speaking your language because you practiced. Action is what makes the difference.

If you do your best in the search for personal freedom, in the search for self-love, you will discover that it's just a matter of time before you find what you are looking for. It's not about daydreaming or sitting for hours dreaming in meditation. You have to stand up and be a human. You have to honor the man or woman that you are. Respect your body, enjoy your body, love your body, feed, clean, and heal your body. Exercise and do what makes your body feel good. This is a *puja* to your body, and that is a communion between you and God.

You don't need to worship idols of the Virgin Mary, the Christ, or the Buddha. You can if you want to; if it feels good, do it. Your own body is a manifestation of God, and if you honor your body everything will change for you. When you practice giving love to every part of your body, you plant seeds of love in your mind, and when they grow, you will love, honor, and respect your body immensely.

Every action then becomes a ritual in which you are honoring God. After that, the next step is honoring God with every thought, every emotion, every belief, even what is "right" or "wrong." Every thought becomes a communion with God, and you will live a dream without judgments, victimization, and free of the need to gossip and abuse yourself.

❧

When you honor these four agreements together, there is no way that you will live in hell.

There is *no way*. If you are impeccable with your word, if you don't take anything personally, if you don't make assumptions, if you always do your best, then you are going to have a beautiful life. You are going to control your life one hundred percent.

The Four Agreements are a summary of the mastery of transformation, one of the masteries of the Toltec. You transform hell into heaven. The dream of the planet is transformed into your personal dream of heaven. The knowledge is there; it's just waiting for you to use it. The Four Agreements are there; you just need to adopt these agreements and respect their meaning and power.

Just do your best to honor these agreements. You can make this agreement today: I choose to honor the Four Agreements. It's so simple and logical that even a child can understand them. But, you must have a very strong will, a very strong will to keep these agreements. Why? Because wherever we go we find that our path is full of obstacles. Everyone tries to sabotage our commitment to these new agreements, and everything around us is a setup for us to break them. The problem is all the other agreements that are a part of the dream of the planet. They are alive, and they are very strong.

That's why you need to be a great hunter, a great warrior, who can defend these Four Agreements with your life. Your happiness, your freedom, your entire way of living depends on it. The warrior's goal is to transcend this world, to escape from this hell, and never come back. As the Toltecs teach us, the reward is to transcend the human experience of suffering, to become the embodiment of God. That is the reward.

We really need to use every bit of power we have to succeed in keeping these agreements. I didn't expect that I could do it at first. I have fallen many times, but I stood up and kept going. And I fell again, and I kept going. I didn't feel sorry for myself. There was no way that I felt sorry for myself. I said, "If I fall, I am strong enough, I'm intelligent enough, I can do it!" I stood up and kept going. I fell and I kept going and going, and each time it became easier and easier. Yet, in the beginning it was so hard, so difficult.

So if you fall, do not judge. Do not give your Judge the satisfaction of turning you into a victim. No, be tough with yourself. Stand up and make the agreement again. "Okay, I broke my agreement to be impeccable with my word. I will start all over again. I am going to keep the Four Agreements just for today. Today I will be impeccable with my word, I will not take anything personally, I will not make any assumptions, and I am going to do my best."

If you break an agreement, begin again tomorrow, and again the next day. It will be difficult at first, but each day will become easier and easier, until someday you will discover that you are ruling your life with these Four Agreements. And, you will be surprised at the way your life has been transformed.

You don't need to be religious or go to church every day. Your love and self-respect are growing and growing. You can do it. If I did it, you can do it also.

Do not be concerned about the future; keep your attention on today, and stay in the present moment. Just live one day at a time. *Always do your best* to keep these agreements, and soon it will be easy for you. Today is the beginning of a new dream.

6

THE TOLTEC PATH TO FREEDOM

Breaking Old Agreements

EVERYONE TALKS ABOUT FREEDOM. ALL AROUND the world different people, different races, different countries are fighting for freedom. But what is freedom? In America we speak of living in a free country. But are we really free? Are we free to be who we really are? The answer is no, we are not free. True freedom has to do with the human spirit — it is the freedom to be who we really are.

Who stops us from being free? We blame the government, we blame the weather, we blame our parents, we blame religion, we blame God. Who really stops us from being free? We stop ourselves. What does it really mean to be free? Sometimes we get married and we say that we lose our freedom, then we get divorced and we are still not free. What stops us? Why can't we be ourselves?

We have memories of long ago, when we used to be free and we loved being free, but we have forgotten what freedom really means.

If we see a child who is two or three, perhaps four years old, we find a free human. Why is this human free? Because this human does whatever he or she wants to do. The human is completely wild. Just like a flower, a tree, or an animal that has not been domesticated — wild! And if we observe humans who are two years old, we find that most of the time these humans have a big smile on their face and they're having fun. They are exploring the world. They are not afraid to play. They are afraid when they are hurt, when they are hungry, when some of their needs are not met, but they don't worry about the past, don't care about the future, and only live in the present moment.

Very young children are not afraid to express what they feel. They are so loving that if they perceive love, they melt into love. They are not afraid to love at all. That is the description of a normal human being. As children we are not afraid of the future or ashamed of the past. Our normal human tendency is to enjoy life, to play, to explore, to be happy, and to love.

But, what has happened with the adult human? Why are we so different? Why are we not wild? From the point of view of the Victim we can say that something sad happened to us, and from the point of view of the warrior we can say that what happened to us is normal. What has happened is that we have the Book of Law, the big Judge and the

Victim who rule our lives. We are no longer free because the Judge, the Victim, and the belief system don't allow us to be who we really are. Once our minds have been programmed with all that garbage, we are no longer happy.

This chain of training from human to human, from generation to generation, is perfectly normal in human society. You don't need to blame your parents for teaching you to be like them. What else could they teach you but what they know? They did the best they could, and if they abused you, it was due to their own domestication, their own fears, their own beliefs. They had no control over the programming they received, so they couldn't have behaved any differently.

There is no need to blame your parents or anyone who abused you in your life, including yourself. But it is time to stop the abuse. It is time to free yourself of the tyranny of the Judge by changing the foundation of your own agreements. It is time to be free from the role of the Victim.

The real you is still a little child who never grew up. Sometimes that little child comes out when you are having fun or playing, when you feel happy, when you are painting, or writing poetry, or playing the piano, or expressing yourself in some way. These are the happiest moments of your life — when the real you comes out, when you don't care about the past and you don't worry about the future. You are childlike.

But there is something that changes all that: We call them *responsibilities*. The Judge says, "Wait a second, you are responsible, you have things to do, you have to work, you have to go to school, you have to earn a living." All these responsibilities come to mind. Our face changes and becomes serious again. If you watch children when they are playing adults, you will see their little faces change. "Let's pretend I'm a lawyer," and right away their faces change; the adult face takes over. We go to court and that is the face we see — and that is what we are. We are still children, but we have lost our freedom.

The freedom we are looking for is the freedom to be ourselves, to express ourselves. But if we look at our lives we will see that most of the time we do things just to please others, just to be accepted by others, rather than living our lives to please ourselves. That is what has happened to our freedom. And we see in our society and all the societies around the world, that for every thousand people, nine hundred and ninety-nine are completely domesticated.

The worst part is that most of us are not even aware that we are not free. There is something inside that whispers to us that we are not free, but we do not understand what it is, and why we are not free.

The problem with most people is that they live their lives and never discover that the Judge and the Victim rule their mind, and therefore they don't have a chance to be free. The first step toward personal freedom is awareness. We need to be aware that we are not free in order to be free. We need to be aware of what the problem is in order to solve the problem.

Awareness is always the first step because if you are not aware, there is nothing you can change. If you are not aware that your mind is full of wounds and emotional poison, you cannot begin to clean and heal the wounds and you will continue to suffer.

There is no reason to suffer. With awareness you can rebel and say, "This is enough!" You can look for a way to heal and transform your personal dream. The dream of the planet is just a dream. It is not even real. If you go into the dream and start challenging your beliefs, you will find that most of the beliefs that guided you into the wounded mind are not even true. You will find that you suffered all those years of drama for nothing. Why? Because the belief system that was put inside your mind is based on lies.

That is why it is important for you to master your own dream; that is why the Toltecs became dream masters. Your life is the manifestation of your dream; it is an art. And you can change your life anytime if you aren't enjoying the dream. Dream masters create a masterpiece of life; they control the dream by making choices. Everything has consequences and a dream master is aware of the consequences.

To be Toltec is a way of life. It is a way of life where there are no leaders and no followers, where you have your own truth and live your own truth. A Toltec becomes wise, becomes wild, and becomes free again.

There are three masteries that lead people to become Toltecs. First is the Mastery of Awareness. This is to be aware of who we really are, with all the possibilities. The second is the Mastery of Transformation — how to change, how to be free of domestication. The third is the Mastery of Intent. Intent from the Toltec point of view is that part of life that makes transformation of energy possible; it is the one living being that seamlessly encompasses all energy, or what we call "God." Intent is life itself; it is unconditional love. The Mastery of Intent is therefore the Mastery of Love.

When we talk about the Toltec path to freedom, we find that they have an entire map for breaking free of domestication. They compare the Judge, the Victim, and the belief system to a parasite that invades the human mind. From the Toltec point of view, all humans who are domesticated are sick. They are sick because there is a parasite that controls the mind and controls the brain. The food for the parasite is the negative emotions that come from fear.

If we look at the description of a parasite, we find that a parasite is a living being who lives off of other living beings, sucking their energy without any useful contribution in return, and hurting their host little by little. The Judge, the Victim, and the belief system fit this description very well. Together they comprise a living being made of psychic or emotional energy, and that energy is alive. Of course it is not material energy, but neither are emotions material energy. Our dreams are not material energy either, but we know they exist.

One function of the brain is to transform material energy into emotional energy. Our brain is the factory of the emotions. And we have said that the main function of the mind is to dream. The Toltecs believe that the parasite — the Judge, the Victim, and the belief system — has control of your mind; it controls your personal dream. The parasite dreams through your mind and lives its life through your body. It survives on the emotions that come from fear, and thrives on drama and suffering.

The freedom we seek is to use our own mind and body, to live our own life, instead of the life of the belief system. When we discover that the mind is controlled by the Judge and the Victim and the real "us" is in the corner, we have just two choices. One choice is to keep living the way we are, to surrender to the Judge and the Victim, to keep living in the dream of the planet. The second choice is to do what we do as children when parents try to domesticate us. We can rebel and say "No!" We can declare a war against the parasite, a war against the Judge and the

Victim, a war for our independence, a war for the right to use our own mind and our own brain.

That is why in all the shamanic traditions in America, from Canada to Argentina, people call themselves *warriors,* because they are in a war against the parasite in the mind. That is the real meaning of a warrior. The warrior is one who rebels against the invasion of the parasite. The warrior rebels and declares a war. But to be a warrior doesn't mean we always win the war; we may win or we may lose, but we always do our best and at least we have a chance to be free again. Choosing this path gives us, at the very least, the dignity of rebellion, and ensures that we will not be the helpless victim of our own whimsical emotions or the poisonous emotions of others. Even if we succumb to the enemy — the parasite — we will not be among those victims who would not fight back.

At best, being a warrior gives us an opportunity to transcend the dream of the planet, and to change our personal dream to a dream that we call *heaven.* Just like hell, heaven is a place that exists within our mind. It is a place of joy, a place where we are happy, where we are free to love and to be who we really are. We can reach heaven while we are alive; we don't have to wait until we die. God is always present and the kingdom of heaven is everywhere, but first we need to have the eyes and ears to see and hear that truth. We need to be free of the parasite.

The parasite can be compared to a monster with a thousand heads. Every head of the parasite is one of the fears that we have. If we want to be free, we have to destroy the parasite. One solution is to attack the parasite head by head, which means we face each of our fears, one by one. This is a slow process, but it works. Every time we face one of the fears we are a little more free.

A second approach is to stop feeding the parasite. If we don't give the parasite any food, we kill the parasite by starvation. To do this we have to gain control of our emotions, we have to refrain from fueling the emotions that come from fear. This is easy to say, but it is very difficult to do. It is difficult because the Judge and the Victim control our mind.

A third solution is called the *initiation of the dead.* The initiation of the dead is found in many traditions and esoteric schools around the world. We find it in Egypt, India, Greece, and America. This is a symbolic death which kills the parasite without harming our physical body. When we "die" symbolically the parasite has to die. This is faster than the first two solutions, but it is even more difficult to do. We need a great deal of courage to face the angel of death. We need to be very strong.

Let's take a closer look at each of these solutions.

THE ART OF TRANSFORMATION: THE DREAM OF THE SECOND ATTENTION

We have learned that the dream you are living now is the result of the outside dream hooking your attention and feeding you all of your beliefs. The process of domestication can be called *the dream of the first attention* because it was how your attention was used for the first time to create the first dream of your life.

One way to change your beliefs is to focus your attention on all those agreements and beliefs, and change the agreements with yourself. In doing this you are using your attention for the second time, thus creating *the dream of the second attention* or the new dream.

The difference is that you are no longer innocent. When you were a child this was not true; you didn't have a choice. But you are no longer a child. Now it's up to you to choose what to believe and what not to believe. You can choose to believe in anything, and that includes believing in yourself.

The first step is to become aware of the fog that is in your mind. You must become aware that you are dreaming all the time. Only with awareness do you have the possibility of transforming your dream. If you have the awareness that the whole drama of your life is the result of what you believe, and what you believe is not real, then you can begin to change it. However, to really change your beliefs you need to focus your attention on what it is that you want to change. You have to know which agreements you want to change before you can change them.

So the next step is to develop awareness of all the self-limiting, fear-based beliefs that make you unhappy. You take an inventory of all that you believe, all your agreements, and through this process you begin the transformation. The Toltecs called this the Art of Transformation, and it's a whole mastery. You achieve the Mastery of Transformation by changing the fear-based agreements that make you suffer, and reprogramming your own mind, in your own way. One of the ways to do this is to explore and adopt alternative beliefs such as the Four Agreements.

The decision to adopt the Four Agreements is a declaration of war to regain your freedom from the parasite. The Four Agreements offer the possibility of ending the emotional pain, which can open the door for you to enjoy your life and begin a new dream. It's up to you to explore the possibilities of your dream, if you are interested. The Four Agreements were created to assist you in the Art of

Transformation, to help you break the limiting agreements, gain more personal power, and become stronger. The stronger you get, the more agreements you can break until the moment comes when you make it to the core of all of those agreements.

Going to the core of those agreements is what I call *going into the desert.* When you go into the desert you meet your demons face-to-face. After coming out of the desert, all those demons become angels.

Practicing the four new agreements is a big act of power. Breaking the spell of black magic in your mind requires great personal power. Every time you break an agreement, you gain extra power. You start by breaking agreements that are very small and require less power. As those smaller agreements are broken, your personal power will increase until you reach a point when you can finally face the big demons in your mind.

For example, the little girl who was told not to sing is now twenty years old and she still does not sing. One way she can overcome the belief that her voice is ugly is to say, "Okay, I will try to sing, even if I do sing badly." Then she can pretend that someone is clapping and telling her, "Oh! That was beautiful." This may break the agreement a teeny, tiny bit, but it will still be there. However, now she has a little more power and courage to try again and again until finally she breaks the agreement.

That's one way out of the dream of hell. But for every agreement you break that makes you suffer, you will need to replace it with a new agreement that makes you happy. This will keep the old agreement from coming back. If you occupy the same space with a new agreement, then the old agreement is gone forever and in its place is the new agreement.

There are many strong beliefs in the mind that can make this process look hopeless. This is why you need to go step-by-step and be patient with yourself because this is a slow process. The way you are living now is the result of many years of domestication. You cannot expect to break the domestication in one day. Breaking agreements is very difficult because we put the power of the word (which is the power of our will) into every agreement we have made.

We need the same amount of power to change an agreement. We cannot change an agreement with less power than we used to make the agreement, and almost all our personal power is invested in keeping the agreements we have with ourselves. That's because our agreements are actually like a strong addiction. We are addicted to being the way we are. We are addicted to anger, jealousy, and self-pity. We are addicted to the beliefs that tell us, "I'm not good enough, I'm not intelligent enough. Why even try? Other people will do it because they're better than me."

All of these old agreements which rule our dream of life are the result of repeating them over and over again. Therefore, to adopt the Four Agreements, you need to put repetition in action. Practicing the new agreements in your life is how your best becomes better. Repetition makes the master.

THE DISCIPLINE OF THE WARRIOR: CONTROLLING YOUR OWN BEHAVIOR

Imagine that you awake early one morning overflowing with enthusiasm for the day. You feel good. You are happy and have plenty of energy to face the day. Then at breakfast, you have a big fight with your spouse, and a flood of emotion comes out. You get mad, and in the emotion of anger you spend a lot of personal power. After the fight, you feel drained, and you just want to go and cry. In fact, you feel so tired that you go to your room, collapse, and try to recover. You spend the day wrapped up in your emotions. You have no energy to keep going, and you just want to walk away from everything.

Every day we awake with a certain amount of mental, emotional, and physical energy that we spend throughout the day. If we allow our emotions to deplete our energy, we have no energy to change our life or to give to others.

The way you see the world will depend upon the emotions you are feeling. When you are angry, everything around you is wrong, nothing is right. You blame everything including the weather; whether it's raining or the sun is shining, nothing pleases you. When you are sad, everything around you is sad and makes you cry. You see the trees and you feel sad; you see the rain and everything looks so sad. Perhaps you feel vulnerable and have a need to protect yourself because you don't know in what moment someone will attack you. You do not trust anything or anyone around you. This is because you see the world with the eyes of fear!

Imagine that the human mind is the same as your skin. You can touch healthy skin and it feels wonderful. Your skin is made for perception and the sensation of touch is wonderful. Now imagine you have an injury and the skin gets cut and infected. If you touch the infected skin, it is going to hurt, so you try to cover and protect the skin. You will not enjoy being touched because it hurts.

Now imagine that all humans have this skin disease. Nobody can touch each other because it is going to hurt. Everyone has wounds on their skin, so the infection is seen as normal, the pain is also considered normal; we believe we are supposed to be that way.

Can you imagine how we would behave with each other if all the humans in the world had this skin disease? Of course we would hardly ever hug each other because it would be too painful. So we would need to create a lot of distance between us.

The human mind is exactly like this description of infected skin. Every human has an emotional body completely covered with infected wounds. Each wound is infected with emotional poison — the poison of all the emotions that makes us suffer, such as hate, anger, envy, and sadness. An action of injustice opens a wound in the mind and we react with emotional poison because of the concepts and beliefs we have about injustice and what is fair. The mind is so wounded and full of poison by the process of domestication, that everyone describes the wounded mind as normal. This is considered normal, but I can tell you it is not normal.

We have a dysfunctional dream of the planet, and humans are mentally sick with a disease called fear. The symptoms of the disease are all the emotions that make humans suffer: anger, hate, sadness, envy, and betrayal. When the fear is too great, the reasoning mind begins to fail, and we call this mental illness. Psychotic behavior occurs when the mind is so frightened and the wounds so painful, that it seems better to break contact with the outside world.

If we can see our state of mind as a disease, we find there is a cure. We don't have to suffer any longer. First we need the truth to open the emotional wounds, take the poison out, and heal the wounds completely. How do we do this? We must forgive those we feel have wronged us, not because they deserve to be forgiven, but because we love ourselves so much we don't want to keep paying for the injustice.

Forgiveness is the only way to heal. We can choose to forgive because we feel compassion for

ourselves. We can let go of the resentment and declare, "That's enough! I will no longer be the big Judge
that goes against myself. I will no longer beat myself
up and abuse myself. I will no longer be the Victim."

First, we need to forgive our parents, our brothers, our sisters, our friends, and God. Once you
forgive God, you can finally forgive yourself. Once
you forgive yourself, the self-rejection in your mind
is over. Self-acceptance begins, and the self-love will
grow so strong that you will finally accept yourself
just the way you are. That's the beginning of the free
human. Forgiveness is the key.

You will know you have forgiven someone when
you see them and you no longer have an emotional
reaction. You will hear the name of the person and
you will have no emotional reaction. When someone
can touch what used to be a wound and it no longer
hurts you, then you know you have truly forgiven.

The truth is like a scalpel. The truth is painful,
because it opens all of the wounds which are covered by lies so that we can be healed. These lies are

what we call *the denial system.* It's a good thing we have the denial system, because it allows us to cover our wounds and still function. But once we no longer have any wounds or any poison, we don't need to lie anymore. We don't need the denial system, because a healthy mind, like healthy skin, can be touched without hurting. It's pleasurable for the mind to be touched when it is clean.

The problem with most people is that they lose control of their emotions. It is the emotions that control the behavior of the human, not the human who controls the emotions. When we lose control we say things that we don't want to say, and do things that we don't want to do. That is why it is so important to be impeccable with our word and to become a spiritual warrior. We must learn to control the emotions so we have enough personal power to change our fear-based agreements, escape from hell, and create our own personal heaven.

How are we to become a warrior? There are certain characteristics of the warrior that are nearly the same around the world. The warrior has awareness. That's very important. We are aware that we are at war, and the war in our minds requires discipline. Not the discipline of a soldier, but the discipline of a warrior. Not the discipline from the outside to tell us what to do and what not to do, but the discipline to be ourselves, no matter what.

The warrior has control. Not control over another human, but control over one's own emotions, control over one's own self. It is when we lose control that we repress the emotions, not when we are in control. The big difference between a warrior and a victim is that the victim represses, and the warrior refrains. Victims repress because they are afraid to show the emotions, afraid to say what they want to say. To refrain is not the same thing as repression. To refrain is to hold the emotions and to express them in the right moment, not before, not later. That is why warriors are impeccable. They have complete control over their own emotions and therefore over their own behavior.

THE INITIATION OF THE DEAD: EMBRACING THE ANGEL OF DEATH

The final way to attain personal freedom is to prepare ourselves for the initiation of the dead, to take death itself as our teacher. What the angel of death can teach us is how to be truly alive. We become aware that we can die at any moment; we have just the present to be alive. The truth is that we don't know if we are going to die tomorrow. Who knows? We have the idea that we have many years in the future. But do we?

If we go to the hospital and the doctor tells us that we have one week to live, what are we going to do? As we have said before, we have two choices. One is to suffer because we are going to die, and to tell everyone, "Poor me, I am going to die," and really create a huge drama. The other choice is to use every moment to be happy, to do what we really enjoy doing. If we only have one week to live, let's enjoy life. Let's be alive. We can say, "I'm going to be myself. No longer am I going to run my life trying to please other people.

No longer am I going to be afraid of what they think about me. What do I care what others think if I am going to die in one week? I'm going to be myself."

The angel of death can teach us to live every day as if it is the last day of our life, as if there may be no tomorrow. We can begin each day by saying, "I am awake, I see the sun. I am going to give my gratitude to the sun and to everything and everyone, because I am still alive. One more day to be myself."

That is the way I see life, that is what the angel of death taught me — to be completely open, to know that there is nothing to be afraid of. And of course I treat the people I love with love because this may be the last day that I can tell you how much I love you. I don't know if I am going to see you again, so I don't want to fight with you.

What if I had a big fight with you and I told you all those emotional poisons that I have against you and you die tomorrow? Oops! Oh my God, the Judge will get me so bad, and I will feel so guilty for everything that I told you. I will even feel guilty for not telling you how much I love you. The love that makes me happy is the love that I can share with you. Why do I need to deny that I love you? It is not important if you love me back. I may die tomorrow or you may die tomorrow. What makes me happy now is to let you know how much I love you.

You can live your life this way. By doing so, you prepare yourself for the initiation of death. What is going to happen in the initiation of death is that the old dream that you have in your mind is going to die forever. Yes, you are going to have memories of the parasite — of the Judge, the Victim, and what you used to believe — but the parasite will be dead.

That is what is going to die in the initiation of death — the parasite. It is not easy to go for the initiation of death because the Judge and the Victim will fight with everything they have. They don't want to die. And we feel we are the ones who are going to die, and we are afraid of this death.

When we live in the dream of the planet, it is as if we are dead. Whoever survives the initiation of the dead receives the most wonderful gift: the resurrection. To receive the resurrection is to arise from the dead, to be alive, to be ourselves again. The resurrection is to be like a child — to be wild and free, but with a difference. The difference is that we have freedom with wisdom instead of innocence. We are able to break our domestication, become free again, and heal our mind. We surrender to the angel of death, knowing that the parasite will die and we will still be alive with a healthy mind and perfect reason. Then we are free to use our own mind and run our own life.

That is what, in the Toltec way, the angel of death teaches us. The angel of death comes to us and says, "You see everything that exists here is mine; it is not yours. Your house, your spouse, your children, your car, your career, your money — everything is mine and I can take it away when I want to, but for now you can use it."

If we surrender to the angel of death we will be happy forever and ever. Why? Because the angel of death takes the past away in order to make it possible for life to continue. For every moment that is past, the angel of death keeps taking the part that is dead and we keep living in the present. The parasite wants us to carry the past with us and that makes it so heavy to be alive. When we try to live in the past, how can we enjoy the present? When we dream of the future, why must we carry the burden of the past? When are we going to live in the present? That is what the angel of death teaches us to do.

7

THE NEW DREAM

Heaven on Earth

I WANT YOU TO FORGET EVERYTHING YOU HAVE learned in your whole life. This is the beginning of a new understanding, a new dream.

The dream you are living is your creation. It is your perception of reality that you can change at any time. You have the power to create hell, and you have the power to create heaven. Why not dream a different dream? Why not use your mind, your imagination, and your emotions to dream heaven?

Just use your imagination and a tremendous thing will happen. Imagine that you have the ability to see the world with different eyes, whenever you choose. Each time you open your eyes, you see the world around you in a different way.

Close your eyes now, and then open them and look outside.

What you will see is love coming out of the trees, love coming out of the sky, love coming out of the light. You will perceive love from everything around you. This is the state of bliss. You perceive love directly from everything, including yourself and other humans. Even when humans are sad or angry, behind these feelings you can see that they are also sending love.

Using your imagination and your new eyes of perception, I want you to see yourself living a new life, a new dream, a life where you don't need to justify your existence and you are free to be who you really are.

Imagine that you have permission to be happy and to really enjoy your life. Your life is free of conflict with yourself and with others.

Imagine living your life without fear of expressing your dreams. You know what you want, what you don't want, and when you want it. You are free to change your life the way you really want to. You are not afraid to ask for what you need, to say yes or no to anything or anyone.

Imagine living your life without the fear of being judged by others. You no longer rule your behavior according to what others may think about you. You are no longer responsible for anyone's opinion. You have no need to control anyone, and no one controls you, either.

Imagine living your life without judging others. You can easily forgive others and let go of any judgments that you have. You don't have the need to be right, and you don't need to make anyone else wrong. You respect yourself and everyone else, and they respect you in return.

Imagine living without the fear of loving and not being loved. You are no longer afraid to be rejected, and you don't have the need to be accepted. You can say "I love you" with no shame or justification. You can walk in the world with your heart completely open, and not be afraid to be hurt.

Imagine living your life without being afraid to take a risk and to explore life. You are not afraid to lose anything. You are not afraid to be alive in the world, and you are not afraid to die.

Imagine that you love yourself just the way you are. You love your body just the way it is, and you love your emotions just the way they are. You know that you are perfect just as you are.

The reason I ask you to imagine these things is because they are all entirely possible! You can live in the state of grace, the state of bliss, the dream of heaven. But in order to experience this dream, you must first understand what it is.

Only love has the ability to put you in that state of bliss. Being in bliss is like being in love. Being in love is like being in bliss. You are floating in the clouds. You are perceiving love wherever you go. It is entirely possible to live this way all the time. It is possible because others have done it and they are no different from you. They live in bliss because they have changed their agreements and are dreaming a different dream.

Once you feel what it means to live in a state of bliss, you will love it. You will know that heaven on earth is truth — that heaven truly exists. Once you know that heaven exists, once you know it is possible to stay there, it's up to you to make the effort to do it. Two thousand years ago, Jesus told us about the kingdom of heaven, the kingdom of love, but hardly anyone was ready to hear this. They said, "What are you talking about? My heart is empty, I don't feel the love that you are talking about; I don't feel the peace that you have." You don't have to do this. Just imagine that his message of love is possible and you will find that it is yours.

The world is very beautiful and very wonderful. Life can be very easy when love is your way of life.

You can be loving all the time. This is your choice. You may not have a reason to love, but you can love because to love makes you so happy. Love in action only produces happiness. Love will give you inner peace. It will change your perception of everything.

You can see everything with the eyes of love. You can be aware that there is love all around you. When you live this way, there is no longer a fog in your mind. The *mitote* has gone on a permanent vacation. This is what humans have been seeking for centuries. For thousands of years we have been searching for happiness. Happiness is the lost paradise. Humans have worked so hard to reach this point, and this is part of the evolution of the mind. This is the future of humanity.

This way of life is possible, and it's in your hands. Moses called it the Promised Land, Buddha called it Nirvana, Jesus called it Heaven, and the Toltecs call it a New Dream. Unfortunately, your identity is mixed with the dream of the planet. All of your beliefs and agreements are there in the fog.

You feel the presence of the parasite and believe it is you. This makes it difficult to let go — to release the parasite and create the space to experience love. You are attached to the Judge, attached to the Victim. Suffering makes you feel safe because you know it so well.

But there is really no reason to suffer. The only reason you suffer is because you choose to suffer. If you look at your life you will find many excuses to suffer, but a good reason to suffer you will not find. The same is true for happiness. The only reason you are happy is because you choose to be happy. Happiness is a choice, and so is suffering.

Maybe we cannot escape from the destiny of the human, but we have a choice: to suffer our destiny or to enjoy our destiny. To suffer, or to love and be happy. To live in hell, or to live in heaven. My choice is to live in heaven. What is yours?

Prayers

PLEASE TAKE A MOMENT TO CLOSE YOUR EYES, OPEN your heart, and feel all the love that comes from your heart.

I want you to join with my words in your mind and in your heart, to feel a very strong connection of love. Together, we are going to do a very special prayer to experience a communion with our Creator.

Focus your attention on your lungs, as if only your lungs exist. Feel the pleasure when your lungs expand to fulfill the biggest need of the human body — to breathe.

Take a deep breath and feel the air as it fills your lungs. Feel how the air is nothing but love. Notice the connection between the air and the lungs, a connection of love. Expand your lungs with air until your body has the need to expel that air. And then exhale, and feel the pleasure again. Because when we fulfill any need of the human body, it gives us pleasure. To breathe gives us much pleasure. Just to breathe is enough for us to always be happy, to enjoy life. Just to be alive is enough. Feel the pleasure to be alive, the pleasure of the feeling of love. . . .

PRAYER FOR FREEDOM

Today, Creator of the Universe, we ask that you come to us and share with us a strong communion of love. We know that your real name is Love, that to have a communion with you means to share the same vibration, the same frequency that you are, because you are the only thing that exists in the universe.

Today, help us to be like you are, to love life, to be life, to be love. Help us to love the way you love, with no conditions, no expectations, no obligations, without any judgment. Help us to love and accept ourselves without any judgment, because when we judge ourselves, we find ourselves guilty and we need to be punished.

Help us to love everything you create unconditionally, especially other human beings, especially those who live around us — all our relatives and people whom we try so hard to love. Because when we reject them, we reject ourselves, and when we reject ourselves, we reject You.

Help us to love others just the way they are with no conditions. Help us to accept them the way they are, without judgment, because if we judge them, we find them guilty, we blame them, and we have the need to punish them.

Today, clean our hearts of any emotional poison that we have, free our minds from any judgment so that we can live in complete peace and complete love.

Today is a very special day. Today we open our hearts to love again so that we can tell each other "I love you," without any fear, and really mean it. Today, we offer ourselves to you. Come to us, use our voices, use our eyes, use our hands, and use our hearts to share ourselves in a communion of love with everyone. Today, Creator, help us to be just like you are. Thank you for everything that we receive this day, especially for the freedom to be who we really are. Amen.

PRAYER FOR LOVE

We are going to share a beautiful dream together — a dream that you will love to have all of the time. In this dream you are in the middle of a beautiful, warm sunny day. You hear the birds, the wind, and a little river. You walk toward the river. At the edge of the river is an old man in meditation, and you see that out of his head comes a beautiful light of different colors. You try not to bother him, but he notices your presence and opens his eyes. He has the kind of eyes that are full of love and a big smile. You ask him how he is able to radiate all that beautiful light. You ask him if he can teach you to do what he is doing. He replies that many, many, years ago he asked the same question of his teacher.

The old man begins to tell you his story: "My teacher opened his chest and took out his heart, and he took a beautiful flame from his heart. Then he opened my chest, opened my heart, and he put that little flame inside it. He put my heart back in my chest, and as soon as my heart was inside me, I felt intense love, because the flame he put in my heart was his own love.

"That flame grew in my heart and became a big, big fire — a fire that doesn't burn, but purifies everything that it touches. And that fire touched each one of the cells of my body, and the cells of my body loved me back. I became one with my body, but my love grew even more. That fire touched every emotion of my mind, and all the emotions transformed into a strong and intense love. And I loved myself, completely and unconditionally.

"But the fire kept burning and I had the need to share my love. I decided to put a little piece of my love in every tree, and the trees loved me back, and I became one with the trees, but my love did not stop, it grew more. I put a piece of love in every flower, in the grass, in the earth and they loved me back, and we became one. And my love grew more and more to love every animal in the world. They responded to my love and they loved me back, and we became one. But my love kept growing and growing.

"I put a piece of my love in every crystal, in every stone in the ground, in the dirt, in the metals, and they loved me back, and I became one with the earth. And then I decided to put my love in the water, in the oceans, in the rivers, in the rain, in the snow. And they loved me back and we became one. And still my love grew more and more. I decided to give my love to the air, to the wind. I felt a strong communion with the earth, with the wind, with the oceans, with nature, and my love grew and grew.

"I turned my head to the sky, to the sun, to the stars, and put a little piece of my love in every star, in the moon, in the sun, and they loved me back. And I became one with the moon and the sun and the stars, and my love kept growing and growing. And I put a little piece of my love in every human, and I became one with the whole of humanity. Wherever I go, whomever I meet, I see myself in their eyes, because I am a part of everything, because I love."

And then the old man opens his own chest, takes out his heart with that beautiful flame inside, and he puts that flame in your heart. And now that love is growing inside of you. Now you are one with the wind, with the water, with the stars, with all of nature, with all animals, and with all humans. You feel the heat and the light emanating from the flame in your heart. Out of your head shines a beautiful light of different colors. You are radiant with the glow of love and you pray:

Thank you, Creator of the Universe, for the gift of life you have given me. Thank you for giving me everything that I have ever truly needed. Thank you for the opportunity to experience this beautiful body and this wonderful mind. Thank you for living inside me with all your love, with your pure and boundless spirit, with your warm and radiant light.

Thank you for using my words, for using my eyes, for using my heart to share your love wherever I go. I love you just the way you are, and because I am your creation, I love myself just the way I am. Help me to keep the love and the peace in my heart and to make that love a new way of life, that I may live in love the rest of my life. Amen.